CHATGPT GARDENING GUIDE

CHATGPT GARDENING GUIDE

Tips for a Flourishing Garden

BILL VINCENT

RWG Publishing

CONTENTS

1	Introduction	1
2	Choosing the Right Plants	3
3	Soil Preparation and Fertilization	5
4	Watering and Irrigation Techniques	7
5	Pest and Disease Control	9
6	Pruning and Trimming	10
7	Mulching and Weed Control	11
8	Sunlight and Shade Considerations	13
9	Seasonal Care and Maintenance	15
10	Companion Planting	16
11	Container Gardening	18
12	Organic Gardening Methods	20
13	Harvesting and Storage	22
14	Tools and Equipment	24
15	Landscaping and Design	26
16	Troubleshooting Common Garden Problems	27

Copyright © 2024 by Bill Vincent

All rights reserved. No part of this book may be reproduced in any manner whatsoever without written permission except in the case of brief quotations embodied in critical articles and reviews.

First Printing, 2024

CHAPTER 1

Introduction

First of all, the best advice I can probably give you is to follow the instructions. Some seeds take three weeks to sprout, while others can take as many as eight weeks. That's one heck of a difference, and it's important to remember that just because one seed takes a certain amount of time to sprout, another of the same type will not. In fact, seeds from the same fruit won't even grow at the same rate. Peppers, for example, have five different types of seeds and the variations can be tremendous. What I remember most is that some chilies will not grow any faster than the tortoise, and there's no use in cooking a grilled cheese if I don't have the tomatoes for it. I will grace you with your bounty when I'm ready—with the combination of sun and moisture levels I need to thrive.

As you've probably noticed, OpenAI has some fun ideas when it comes to the prompts for ChatGPT: artificial intelligence and poetry go together like beans and the trellis, don't you think! I tend to think they do a good job being creative about thinking up prompts, and when I saw the one that said, "What advice would you give someone who's struggling to get all the plants in their garden to flourish?" I thought, "I got this." I've been gardening for the last two years, and while I'm no expert, I may be able to offer some advice. I'll assume that you're already doing some of the obvious things, like weeding, watering, and providing enough light. So, here you go: ChatGPT's guide to growing your plants!

CHAPTER 2

Choosing the Right Plants

This is especially important if you are a first-time gardener. If you are an experienced gardener, you can take more risks, but it is generally best to start with a plot that is not too ambitious. Plant your garden in an area that receives plenty of sunlight. Most edible plants require 6-8 hours of direct sunlight per day. If your garden is not in the 6-8 hour window, try to trim trees or install a trellis in the upper area placed in a sunnier place. A garden that is shaded up to the ankle of a tree or the wall of a house may require a trellis to capture sunlight from where it is located. A garden with dappled sunlight may still produce fewer crops than a garden with full sun, but it will still be productive with the right crops and boundaries. A garden with full or almost full shade will have limited planting options.

- Peace lilies: Peace lilies are the perfect plant to start your collection. They thrive in a variety of lighting conditions, including low light. - Snake plants: This hardy plant is almost indestructible. It adapts to a variety of lighting conditions and needs water only when the soil is dry. - Aloe vera: This plant not only looks good on a windowsill, it is also useful. It thrives on neglect, so it is perfect for forgetfulness or a lack of care.

If you want your garden to succeed and not become a pit of fear and worry, choose the right plants from the very beginning. Why wouldn't these be the ones that seem interesting and beautiful? In fact, you may want to grow plants that require more care, water, and light than you can provide. With all the care in the world, you still may not succeed.

CHAPTER 3

Soil Preparation and Fertilization

Soil preparation should normally begin several months before planting. Some trees have broad, impenetrable root systems that are mingled into p.ie. by deep soil work up to 18 inches (46 cm) deep. Other trees, such as magnolias, have roots that are buried near the surface. Deep soil work up to 10 inches (25 cm) deep, the hoe hand has done a comprehensive handling thoroughly. The next phase of the preparation may include Brooks mountain inspecting, coconut coatings, and caswading, followed by a further comprehensive arrangement. Where the ground level will be changed, direct planting work follows the soil pattern. For a single-crop approach, discard two-meter long strips of ground for each plant of the same species. If the plants are not known areas. The first days of this earth, then completely clean up arrows for 50–70 cm long and from row.

From the first time we lay it to rest, soil begins a remarkable system of relationships. It gives us food and shelter, the raw materials and the energy for life, and an extraordinary exposed field as a space for a variety of forms to antagonize, collaborate, and reconnect. At the same time, we are now beginning to understand the existence and roles of the invisible networks involved in the construction of these loose material features supporting these vital soil functions. Plants need the structurally strong support and nutrients we call soil, but its formation itself depends on the growth of its roots. Understanding these co-evolutionary interactions is critical to maintain the vital functions that soil provides in terms of subsurface forests, transfer of water and other assets and requirements of life, nutrient storage, and terraces for capturing the global greenhouse gas carbon in time we want to tackle and manage the major challenges.

CHAPTER 4

Watering and Irrigation Techniques

To avoid over- or underwatering your plants, provide the right amount of water at the right time of day. The best time of day to water plants is early in the morning. The soil has been cooled off by the nighttime, and the water can seep in deep before evaporating. This also opens the plants' stomata to ingest a good amount of water and nutrients. It also lowers the moisture levels around the leaves, reducing moisture-loving plant diseases. The plants do not become very cold, and roots are less likely to freeze if planted in a cooler climate. They are also less likely to get sunburned. If you cannot water your plants in the morning, then in the late afternoon is the second-best time. Water that has a heat buildup is replaced by cooler water, oxygenating the roots. Watering during this time also helps the plants survive the heat of the day, and they can conserve water. If given the correct amount of water, plants will show supple branches, are easy to manipulate, contain a good amount of moisture, and can survive the heat, the wind, and cool nights.

What the right amount of watering does for your garden: Adequate water for plants is the driving force behind the transpirational flow of nutrients from the soil. If the soil is not moist enough, the leaves and stems of most plants will not form properly. For instance, the leaves of a tomato plant will show a curling pattern, and the leaves of a pepper plant will show a type of black purplish hue. The overall growth of the plants will be stunted if the temperatures are warmer than 85 degrees Fahrenheit, or the plants might not produce any fruit. If a mature plant does not get enough water, it will show wilting signs, such as on zucchinis, tomatoes, or okras. It will also not recover when it is cooler. In contrast, if the plants are watered properly, they will provide a good fruit yield. Too much water can result from the excessive use of a fertilizer, which turns into salts and draws water from the cells. When the cells are depleted of water, the plant wilts. If the plants are watered excessively, the roots die at the tips, turning into a brownish color and soft to the touch.

CHAPTER 5

Pest and Disease Control

Plant diseases are often difficult to diagnose. Environmental conditions impact plant health more than any other factor, so proper investigation is required for accurate control strategies. A good rule of thumb to help control disease issues is to keep your plant healthy by managing soil fertility, planting time, and good watering management practices. Ensure adequate spacing, prune plants, and manage weeds. Reduce stress on your plants.

Regular observation and spending a bit of time in your garden is the first line of defense, ensuring timely and appropriate response. Knowledge of the beneficial insects and other organisms will go a long way toward managing and reducing harmful ones. If further assistance is needed, contact the entomologist at your state or land grant university.

One of the most difficult parts about growing a garden is the opportunity for disease, weeds, and pests to get in your plants and harm them before you have the chance to reap the rewards of all your hard work. Protect your plants with these gardening group expert tips. Keeping good records from year to year and knowing your plants' growth patterns will help you be prepared. Life cycles of pests can also be interrupted and managed once you know what to look for and the strategies to manage.

CHAPTER 6

Pruning and Trimming

Trimming is just as important. Trimming consists of reducing your plants' foliage to better air circulation and improve photosynthesis. Don't worry about the plants, they will grow back with a vengeance! Always make sure a large amount of the leaf is still left in place. If you go too tight, they might think they need to produce more dense foliage and fewer flowers. Not what you are after. Never trim a sun-starved plant. Only trim if the plant is in direct sunlight or has excellent grow lights and a good LED setup. Never trim your chilies and aubergines, they love their leaves and need them! I use this guide from Leafy houseplants to determine if I should trim a specific plant or not.

When it's time for pruning, never cut too many leaves at once. It freaks out your plant, encourages pests and disease, and slows down transpiration and photosynthesis, ultimately reducing the rate of fruit ripening. Carefully select the saddest and oldest looking leaves or stems and remove no more than 20% of those at each sitting. Also, avoid cutting your plants at the nodes on the main stem - this will slow down their growth and vigor. I learned the hard way - never cut the production plant. This includes chilies and aubergines. Only tuck away the taller top leaves if they get in the way or are small. Here is a great detailed guide on what to trim in your plant.

CHAPTER 7

Mulching and Weed Control

Weeds require space, color, and nutrition in order to grow. In soil, weeds cannot always survive. To avoid weeds, a combination of strategies and regular care of a piece contains all of these essential components, but the ultimate objective is the avoidance of unsatisfied gaps by means of control of soil and crops. Weeds have the opportunity in your garden when the ground's discovery is focused and personalized gardening can negate about 80 percent of the need for synthetic and organic grown products. When treating saplings, individual garden beds are monitored for the placement of mulch, and the inclusion of decapitated scrub trees, branches, and leaves. Rich soil preparation is also an essential step to avoid cultivated spaces, to ensure that weeds occurring right there are drawn up against shallow and easily exposed baby roots.

The majority of healthy plant growth and development is a result of the equilibrium in the soil. Crushed leaves, wood chips, and bark products all degrade above the soil, enriching and providing nutrient requirements to vigorous plants with time. Over a garden bed covered with mulch, you can place up to 100 layers of newspaper (no glossy or colored sections). Search advertisements and scrap paper are others. Mulch will prevent the warmth of the sun from producing weed seed germination, while also respecting its planting system, stopping the roots and ensuring no mulch is turned away from the stalk.

CHAPTER 8

Sunlight and Shade Considerations

You miss the early day sunlight, morning sunlight, midday or high sun to free the dreams of the flowers, noontime sunlight, midsummer sunlight, evening sunlight as the shade is tracked, and maybe even night light, moonlight when it can fall. Furthermore, these words of wisdom certainly can apply to flower, vegetable, or fruit garden. Eyeing really does not stop before a majority of the garden species. Actually, the meadow applies in the exact same way more. Perennials again will not look favorably upon the idea of any amount of either thatching or watering; and two trees are trees, and that only ends the forest.

Of course, the most vital aspect of gardening that goes so unmentioned is sunlight. Actually, shade is spoken about all the time, so there's something seriously wrong if important information is not being supplemented in the discussion about shade. Actually, shade should be completely and totally ignored. There is a consensus that no actual shade plant is being considered in garden discussion. So the whole story begins with sunlight. Sunlight is the ongoing question in every garden from the North Pole to the South Pole, from the Equator in Ecuador and but no surrounding ice. Hopefully, the land is poor enough, and the sunshine is strong and plentiful to actually grow any sort of plant, and actually live on it. Our ancestors knew how to figure that out, and even folks nowadays can figure that out too.

CHAPTER 9

Seasonal Care and Maintenance

I would be wanting your fruit trees that need pruning right now, is from January to February, very early March is your time that you should be doing that so that's your bare rooted time that you can grab them. It's the best time that things will take their root from there and right now because January is upon us that's when you want and in February get those guys pruned and they're really easy. If you're new to fruit trees, I've got a really simple video that Jord's got to put together for you in a link down below that shows you very simple steps of how to prune an Espaliered fruit tree, so keep an eye out for the website when you're looking for the videos that you're interested in.

Depending on your climate zone, there will be some seasonal things to look after and you don't need to worry about this pruned in late winter and the early spring, and that's when they're at their dormancy. It is best to do them when it doesn't freeze, in late winter and early spring in parts of the world that get a freeze. Like I mentioned, if you're in California and you're in Orange County and parts in that general area.

CHAPTER 10

Companion Planting

Cabbage, potatoes, broad beans, spinach, or celery - These help shade one another's roots while occupying different soil layers. Plant them in a polyculture with leafy greens. Beans and potatoes - Beans don't take up much space, leaving room for potatoes below the soil. The lanky beans also provide some shade for the potatoes. Cucumbers and nasturtiums - Plant this flower as a barrier around your cucumbers to repel aphids. Radishes, cucumbers, lettuces, carrots, or peas - Radishes germinate quickly and can be used as a border crop to control power-driven weeds. Their leaves and roots also act as a trap crop for flea beetles. Carrots and leeks - Together, they repel each other's pests. Onions and carrots grow well together. Dill, fennel, and marigolds - These help protect plants from insects and stimulate general growth. Dill is a great herb to have around your squash, cucumbers, and onions. Common dill pests are aphids and cabbage loppers. Fennel also helps deter Japanese beetles and snails. Marigolds can deter nematodes and give each of your plant's roots a layer of protection. They also repel squash vine borers and cucumber beetles.

Common companion planting combos:

Companion planting is an amazing natural way to increase your yield, reduce pest problems, and nurture a healthy ecosystem. Experimenting with companion planting can be a lot of fun as you try to find the best plant combos that work for your garden. We've detailed some companion plant options in previous plant-specific articles, but here we'll focus on a more general guide.

CHAPTER 11

Container Gardening

The outcome depends on the measurement of your tubing. Containers are restricting the horizontal spread of root systems, so deep, loose soil is required to accommodate these root designs. This usually dictates a width of 45 to 60 cm (18 to 24 inches). Upside pots with a larger diameter and just grasses and tall flowers should be provided with sufficiently wide pots. The only condition is that the pots must retain water so they don't dry out easily due to evaporation. The taller a plant, the greater the weight of a pot. Soil surfaces should be grouped with small pots inside larger pots. This has a similar effect on potted plants as wall lining in shell buildings, insulating them in extreme temperatures. With a lot of time on their hands, it is essential to have the option of allowing DIY-ers, especially this course, or that unique built-in touch to use almost everything.

You can container-plant a huge variety of fruits, vegetables, herbs, shrubs, and trees in pots. Pots are readily available and easy to move around, and you can grow several things in one container. Tomato plants and herbs are especially productive in containers. Pots also are great in small urban gardens since they increase your growing space by providing planting areas alongside railings, tables, stairways, and walls. Potted plants dress up patios and balconies, and allow for gardening regardless of the quality of the soil below the paving. Urban planters allow you to raise varying heights (short plants to towering bamboo) and department store rolling racks can help protect gardens or provide separation in common areas of your kitchen. Containers can be placed to isolate exotic and unusual tropical and succulent plants that aren't simultaneously hardy enough to withstand the cold. In pots, you can group together different types of herbs allowing you to experience all bouquets anywhere. A garden packaged in a pot drinks your hard-earned wine.

CHAPTER 12

Organic Gardening Methods

One of the essentials to making an organic garden work for you are beneficial insects. They can protect your garden from environmental damage. So, how do you attract and maintain a beneficial insect population? A good way to start is to plant a few different kinds of nectar-producing or pollen-producing plants near your garden. Another tip is to keep the flowers blooming at all times in the spring, summer and fall. Finally, a good way to maintain beneficial insects is to resist the temptation to use pesticides. Don't forget, organic gardening essentially means building and maintaining your garden soil by working with nature. Why not let nature grow food for you while you sit back and enjoy the garden?

When using organic gardening methods, you're helping the environment by using less energy and ingesting fewer pesticides. Plus, there are some other impressive benefits to organic gardening, including conservation of water and reduction of soil erosion. You are doing your part to help out as well by preserving topsoil through no-till/minimum-till agriculture practices that result in significantly less soil erosion. On top of that, your crops will be better able to resist pests and diseases, which means even less use of chemicals. Overall, organic functions as a way to protect the fertility of your garden while conserving and protecting our environment.

Organic gardening is something that's seeing a boom in popularity, for a number of reasons. It's a hobby that takes you outdoors and allows you to get some fresh air and sunshine. It's a fun and rewarding way to exercise, allows you to harvest something delicious all while reducing waste and chemicals in your environment.

CHAPTER 13

Harvesting and Storage

Clean the harvested vegetables using water or a stiff brush as needed. Don't wash root crops or squash. For the best texture and flavor, cook most vegetables soon after picking. All vegetables and fruits contain enzymes that could cause them to lose flavor and color. Squash, pumpkins, and sweet potatoes, as well as gourds and some root crops and fruits, will store for a longer time under the right conditions. Only store perfect, unblemished, undamaged fruits or vegetables. Store fresh items like carrots, sweet potatoes, parsnips, and turnips in our climate-controlled environment. A damp or humid space with slight air flow is ideal. If the air is too dry, roots will wrinkle. Newspapers or paper bags work well for keeping roots. Fruits, especially apples and pears, should be kept refrigerated. Heirloom varieties are best. Keep fruits away from veggies, especially onions, since their gases will spoil the fruit.

Harvesting and Storage: You've been growing your crops for a while now. It's probably time to get out into the garden and bring in the fruits of your labors. Most vegetables are at the right stage to harvest soon after they reach their mature size. Use the maturity days for each crop as a guideline. Tastes vary, so you can pick while younger or older if you prefer that tenderness. With vine crops, frequent picking is important. Plants stop forming new flowers or fruits if mature ones are left on the plant. Leafy greens, herbs, and fruits like corn should be used or preserved within a few days after picking while vegetables like cucumbers, squash, and okra will keep longer. For the longest shelf life possible, here are some tips. First, use the right tool. Pruners or garden scissors help avoid damaging the plant or the vegetable. Second, picking early and often to keep plants productive. Third, remove the vines or plants. That also helps keep the garden clean.

CHAPTER 14

Tools and Equipment

However, having picked holes in the importance of certain gardening gadgets, there are still some really useful tools and pieces of equipment (for example a watering can or a wheelbarrow) that you will be glad you own before the season is over. It is interesting to note that while no single tool or piece of equipment makes your gardening experience 70% better, every single uninspiring piece of equipment can make your gardening experience 1% better all told. Likewise, not only do we believe that the difficult part is trying to figure out a way to do something that you can't find or afford a tool or piece of equipment for, but we also make it a policy to avoid suggesting anyone spend money on anything that costs over $60 when attempting to offer a cost-cutting alternative to one of high technologies plans. But still, we do think that even if you don't have specialized tools for gardening, but just a die-hard boring kind of shovel to use, you'll find that there is some value in turning over a neglected patch of ground with one that's still not broke.

Having reviewed so many ways to make gardening easier, we'd be remiss if we didn't say that as with most things in life, it's not always necessary to have just the right tool for the job. To be sure, injustice is done when a really good tool is replaced by something that doesn't work so well. Still, if you don't have a lot of money or time to spend on your hobby, it's probably a better plan to find a way to do a task that's a bit less good with a tool or method you can afford, rather than to make do and invent pronouncements about a tool's utility based on a comment read in a gardening catalog or a Facebook post, or the work of an author selling his gardening advice for money. Where would we be if most of the gardeners who came before us said ungracious things about recently invented tools? Also think about gardening in large areas with minimal tools in mind. That's the most efficient approach of them all. And there's less to break too.

CHAPTER 15

Landscaping and Design

Landscaping or gardening is carried out for various reasons: to add beauty to the surroundings, to produce the effect of quiet in contrast to city life, as well as adding value and benefits to the land. To get better long-term benefits, we try to show some landscaping tips that must be followed for better results. Keep the lawn shape as a simple form. Keep it oval or rectangular. Do not shape the irregular edges. Planting near the outer walls of small evergreen shrubs creates a sense of unity with the building, and foundation plantings make the house/institution appear permanent and establish continuity. Keep local reference lines within the property line, especially where the lawn is bordered by main roads, walkways, and driveways.

"Landscaping" means development and design to create a pleasing outdoor environment that is not only functional but also attractive and aesthetic. Landscaping and designing your area or garden around your home gives that finishing touch and leaves a good impression on your guests. The idea of landscaping is to develop and give an aesthetic finish to exterior land, with trees, plants, grasses, flowers, as well as adding other structures and decorative objects.

CHAPTER 16

Troubleshooting Common Garden Problems

Water: Over-watering makes the delicate roots of the plant break down, making the plant suffocate and the mold rot. Lack of water can make a plant dehydrated and cause similar leaves. The amount of water your plant needs depends on the soil and plant species, but it is generally unacceptable to let your plant dry between watering. You may need to water some plant species every 2-3 days. You can reduce the frequency of watering every 2-3 weeks to induce better root growth by slightly deepening the roots of the plant, especially if you have a plant outside or facing full sunlight."

16.1 Soil pH Balance: Soil pH imbalance makes it difficult for nutrients to enter the plant through their roots. Unless you adjust the understanding of pH, plants appear sick, their growth becomes weaker and makes them more susceptible to pests and diseases. The pH scale equation is 1-14, with 7 being neutral. Most plants need soil with a pH of 6-7. To measure pH, there are soil testing kits or you can send away specimens plants.

"It's distressing to wake up one morning and find that your plants have grown poorly, drooped, or littered with holes. Gardening is prone to problem-solving because technological constraints always put outdoor plants out of favor. If you're trying to figure out what's going on with your garden, here are your biggest sources of corruption - and what you can do about it.

Milton Keynes UK
Ingram Content Group UK Ltd.
UKHW030908271124
451618UK00011B/336